Guided Scribes & Insights

with
Love & Light

Samantha J Merrigan

BALBOA.
PRESS

A DIVISION OF HAY HOUSE

Balboa Press books may be ordered through booksellers or by contacting:

Balboa Press
A Division of Hay House
1663 Liberty Drive
Bloomington, IN 47403
www.balboapress.com.au
1-(877) 407-4847

ISBN: 978-1-4525-0768-2 (sc)
ISBN: 978-1-4525-0769-9 (e)

Printed in the United States of America

Balboa Press rev. date: 10/19/2012

Everyday tell your-self, I am here to complete a mission on earth, I have a purpose. Open my eyes and my heart and show me which paths to seek.

When we walk in truth and follow our truth, not allowing nothing or no one to divert this truth. It is then we are walking the path to soul growth and Universal blessings each step of the way.

Always be open to see signs and symbols, your angels and guides want you to awaken to their presences each step of your journey.

Give gratitude and be open to receive, in turn giving you purpose and a life of abundance to live.

He who believes and takes action creates a masterpiece of his own manifestations.

*The canvas of life is within your
own creation, when you seek
the creation within, you expand
to greater inner wisdom.*

Walk in your own soul spark and allow it to shine for all to see.

You are approaching a path of walking in your truth now and beginning to open new doors to the meaning of your purpose.

*All you have endured in this life,
thus far, have been soul growths for
you to expand yourself and evolve
on deeper and greater levels.*

Changing your viewpoint of your
fears and walking through them, brings
great personal sense of realisation.

Releasing past pains and fears will give you clear insights and assist in your advancement on a soul level.

Walk with your inner guiding light . . . Say to yourself . . . I am love, I am light, see it, feel it and believe it to be true . . . .

To feel love and share love with another, teaches us about who we truly are, our inner creation evolves and expands to deeper discoveries.

To know love is to share love;
to be love is to feel love.

Love is the key to opening the
doorways to one's inner reality.

Love is the answer to all
healing and awakenings.

Love is who we are intended to be.
Love is what we all strive to become.

The evolution and growth of the individual will attract the soul level of love desired, to further expand and grow ones existence.

A soul mate will assist igniting the spark of your soul and fuel your inner flame.

Understanding love is the fundamental truth to happy relationships with all others. Understanding who you are and your soul purpose to inner truth brings understanding of love; one must first know one self to find peace within, enabling one to openly connect with another unconditionally.

*The key to soul mate love is to first
know thy self with acceptance and love,
unconditional acceptance of another,
open communication expressing feelings
and beliefs without judgement.*

Life begins each passing moment of everyday. Each moment of every passing day is what we choose our life to be. Life is a blessing, life is a gift, life is precious, life is breath, and life is love.

*When you feel down and everyone
around you just doesn't understand,
walk hand in hand with love and faith
and listen to the inner command.*

*Those who speak kindly and project
love to all humanity, will gain greater
wisdom, insights and acceptability.*

Life is breath of love, death is
transformation of deeds done and
undone, pave the ways don't delay,
procrastination will cause dismay.

To be open to giving may be something which makes you feel alive. He, who believes and takes action, creates a masterpiece of his own geniality.

Life brings forth many painful awakenings and can be hard to bare; it's what we do with these that determine where they will lead us.

Ego is something we all have a continual battle with daily, in time, you will be able to defeat it with comfort . . .

We all have free will to choose certain paths and thoughts. If within we know something feels wrong, then it can't be right for our higher purpose . . . can it?

Look back and review, accept what
you feel serves you; leave behind
what you feel does not serve you.

When it feels right it is exactly as your soul needs and desires, listen to this without question, and trust this with conviction.

In denying one, of knowing oneself,
makes you live in an existence
that isn't your own reality.

*When one believes in self, one's
own abilities are endless.*

*No one is above or below another
we are all equal and worthy
of love and acceptance.*

If we don't love and accept ourselves how can we love and accept others within our lives.

Drama does not serve ones path
to evolution, it creates chaos and
confusion, look instead for a
harmonious soul solution.

*Transformation is within
your own creation.*

The energy of what one connects to is what one will be and become.

We are all here to evolve on a soul
level, to complete ones lessons, to
grow deeper on a spiritual level.

There are many pathways we can
take to advance one's own soul growth,
sometimes we make the same mistakes
over and over again, until we receive
and understand the intended lesson.

The present moment is what we are viewing now on an individualistic level. The now moment is important to each person, this brings forth the soul advancement and growths.

Visualisation brings abundance with the guidance of angels and realisation.

What looks invisible can be visible,
if you open your insight, to see
clearly your own inspiration.

The key to completing ones soul path is to always 'listen to the inner voice' and to follow the truth of ones feelings and inner knowing.

If you feel within a resistance, listen to your inner guidance, shift the energy to allow the connection to flow.

Today is the day I find my way,
tomorrow has not yet come, so for
now, I am exactly where I belong.

Those who refrain from bitterness
and resentment will endeavour
to sustain greater wisdom.

Only as strong as I believe, can I find me, only as long as I accept me, it is then I will be set free.

*Imagine being who you want
to be and shaping miraculous
dreams to your own reality.*

One must know what failure feels like to understand the true meaning of success.

Awaken to the endless flow of love and healing energies.

Choices and experiences lead to one's destiny, one can choose which path to take at any given moment, our destinies are not clearly placed in front of us, we make the choices, and how we get there is free will and individual experiencing.

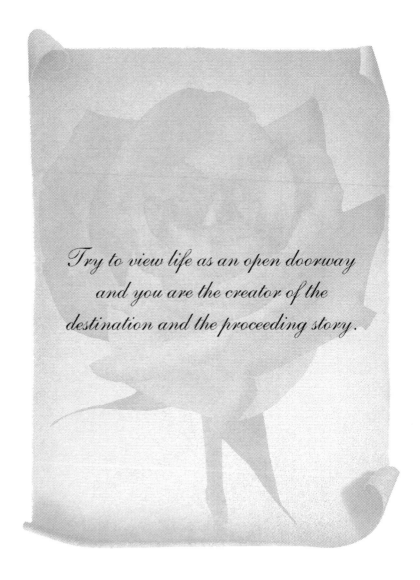

Try to view life as an open doorway and you are the creator of the destination and the proceeding story.

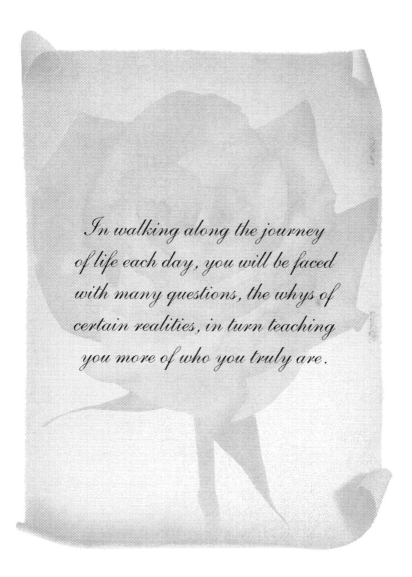

*In walking along the journey
of life each day, you will be faced
with many questions, the whys of
certain realities, in turn teaching
you more of who you truly are.*

He who procrastinates never believes in his own abilities.

Every action has a consequence, every feeling has a meaning, and every wrong doing will come back upon you.

I wonder why some people conform to belong, when one can only be happy when one is truthful to thy self.

To know what ones destiny is and can become, one must first know oneself.

Remove the masks and be yourself, then you will walk a path to happiness, never be like no other for you are special.

We all have free will to choose our
life path along the way, and it is these
choices, which will pave the way, offering
soul lessons each step along the way.

*Today is here; time to inspire
your true desire.*

There may be multitude and
magnitude, but we have the power
within solitude to create attitude.

Silence and wonder can lead
you to opening more doorways,
opening your mind and vision,
brings forth a clearer intention.

Peace of mind brings clarity, you are the master of your own reality, you choose.

As the breeze gently whispers your name, caresses your senses, messages from above, sending sweet love.

*With every experience
comes an awakening.*

Look within and you shall discover
many dimensions connected to your
own individual awakenings.

Open your senses, develop your gifts, look at the beauty of your existence, be open and see the light.

Creation with intent brings success and manifestation of dreams into reality.

*Manifest your life's journey
and inspire your spirit to deliver
the content of the intention.*

For where there is a will, you can become who you want to be, and openly share with all others to see.

We create our own destiny, when
we choose the path of soul integrity,
we hold the key to growth and truth,
we are exactly who we want to be.

Today is the day I find my way,
tomorrow has not yet come, so for
now I see where I belong.

In passing, we are given a new life and transformation to greater soul evolution.

There is no end; there are only processes to greater soul growths, awakenings and continual transformation.

Life is full of awakenings,
opening the treasure within;
life is love, light and truth.

Experiences are the keys to gaining insights.

When you learn to trust what will be, will be, and believe that all which happens in your life, is for a purpose and reason. The outcomes are not what matters; it's the moments in the now. You are being guided to just go with what comes forth in the now and believe in your feelings and your worthiness to receive the love you desire.

You can choose and change how
you feel with a click of a finger.
Choices are there to be made and
decisions will pave your way.

You hold the insights within you,
even when pain arises so deeply,
you can choose to remain captive or
awaken the gifts bestowed upon you.

The road to happiness begins when you follow your own truth, and listen to your inner calling.

There is no one external source one can attach to in finding happiness, if one hasn't connected to the truth within one's own self. The internal essences of your soul being in finding the creation within, can then radiate the love and energy to bring forth the complimentary soul connection with others to ascension.

What is this thing call wisdom
where does it hide?

It comes to you when you
look completely inside.

We all have this within us, little
be—known, Just comes from a
place most call the unknown.

I was lost one day and found my way,
searching for answers it began with a
feeling, now I have found the meaning.

Happiness awaits you if you want it, abundance won't forsake you if you believe, and nothing and no one can harm you unless you surrender your power.

The now is what you create the rest of your path to become. The now matters as each step you take now, will build the foundations of what's to come. Listen to your thoughts and awaken the soul essence of who you want to be and what you want to become.

I am the creator of my life and with my choices; I create what my path is and will become and set my spirit free.

Time passes so quickly; each day
is something which comes and goes.
Don't walk too briskly; for you
must learn to go with the flow.

When you awake; be thankful you have
life, and begin to create. Each moment
is precious; each step you take. Never
look back for nothing is a mistake.

Call upon your helpers, angels
and guides, when you ask for their
guidance; they will walk by your
side. All in good time manifest those
dreams be sure to believe. Then you
will walk in light which will beam.

Dreams are the inner view of who you truly are, your truth in discovering your higher purpose.

The dreamer who awakens to the messages opens the dimensions of one's true reality.

Unlocking the code within your dreams helps you to co-create the masterpiece of your existence and imagination touched with reality.

Within you lies the truth of who
you are, within you is the light
of your being, within you is a
wealth of things yet unseen.

Contact the author:

Samantha Merrigan
PO Box 5274
North Geelong, 3215
Australia.
Phone: 61 3 52771230
Mobile: 61 412706257

www.psychic-awakenings.com